SCIENCE ALLIAN

Willie gets wild about Weather!

by Carole Marsh

© 2011 Carole Marsh

Permission is hereby granted to the individual purchaser or classroom teacher to reproduce materials in this book for non-commercial individual or classroom use only. Reproduction of these materials for an entire school or school system is strictly prohibited.

Gallopade is proud to be a member of these educational organizations and associations.

National Science Teachers Association
The National School Supply and Equipment Association
The National Council for the Social Studies
American Booksellers Association
American Library Association
International Reading Association
National Association for Gifted Children
Museum Store Association
Association of Partners for Public Lands
Association of Booksellers for Children

GALLOPADE INTERNATIONAL

Managing Editor: Sherry Moss
Assistant Editor: Michael Kelly
Senior Editor: Janice Baker
Cover Design: Vicki DeJoy
Content Design: Randolyn Friedlander

Although most of the experiments in this book are regarded as low hazard, author and publisher expressly disclaim all liability for any occurrence, including, but not limited to, damage, injury or death which might arise as consequences of the use of any experiment(s) listed or described here. Therefore, you assume all the liability and use these experiments at your own risk. Author and publisher recommend that all experiments be performed under adult supervision.

Other Books In The Series

- Molly Attracts Opposites with Magnetism!
- Ellie Gets Charged about Electricity!
- Lara Looks at Light and Color!
- Steven Soars into Space Science!
- Eddie Explores Ecosystems and the Food Chain!
- Sam Tunes In to the Science of Sound!
- Mandy Mixes It Up with States of Matter! Solids! Liquids! Gases!
- Robby Unearths Rocks and Minerals!
- Fred Investigates Force and Motion! Includes Simple Machines
- Hannah Hunts for Habitats!
- Gina Discovers Genetics, Characteristics and DNA!
- Luke Surveys Landforms!
- Nick Navigates Natural Disasters!
- Christina Examines Plant Cells and Animal Cells!
- Nina Learns to Appreciate Natural Resources and Conservation!

©Carole Marsh/Gallopade International • www.gallopade.com • Willie gets wild about Weather!

Table of Contents

A Word From Science Alliance...

Hi, Friends!

Welcome to the SCIENCE ALLIANCE!

What's that? We're a group of kids from all over who love science!

We live...eat...breathe science!

We love to read about, go see, experiment, and otherwise immerse ourselves in all kinds of science!

We figure that the future of the earth and our world is pretty much up to us, right? And so, it just seems like knowing a lot about science will help us take better care of our bodies, our land, our water, and our tomorrows!

But, today: Get busy and read this book! It's a lotta fun. We helped write it; we always do! After all, the author, Carole Marsh, is a really great writer...but she's sorta wimpy when it comes to blood, electricity, or experiments in the lab, so we have to help her out.

Ok, we'll be waiting for you inside! And, by the way, welcome to the SCIENCE ALLIANCE!

Lara Molly Nick Willie Robby Eddie Christina Sam Hannah Luke Fred Steven Ellie Gina Mandy Nina

©Carole Marsh/Gallopade International • www.gallopade.com • Willie gets wild about Weather!

A Word From ...
Carole Marsh

Ok, here's the Real Deal:

SCIENCE is fascinating, fun, wild, crazy, easy, hard, mind-blowing, (sometimes lab-blowing!)—and, ESSENTIAL!

In school, you learn to read, you learn to write, and you learn to add and subtract. Those are essential skills! You also learn about the past as you study history and geography.

Science is about the future! And the present! It affects your life each and every minute of each and every day. It always will. It does not matter if you plan to grow up and become a teacher, doctor, lawyer, computer analyst, or anything else—you still MUST know a lot about science.

Science is biology and electricity and windmills and oil deep in the earth and the aurora borealis (Northern Lights) blazing in the sky. Science keeps us warm or makes us cold. It makes our lives easier and better—or, exceedingly miserable!

Science is a study, a tool, a way and a means...it's global warming and Antarctic freezing. It's inside the body and outside the universe. Science is the key to the future. It's the answer to many problems. It's the cutting edge of the cutting edge!

If you don't learn science, you'll be in the dark. You'll also miss out on some amazing, fascinating, funny, mind-blowing, (NO lab-blowing, now—gotta promise!) facts, stories, experiments, and much more.

When you learn about science, you learn about yourself and your world.
So JOIN THE SCIENCE ALLIANCE—and let's do science!

I can't wait!

Carole Marsh
Science Alliance Member Number 1

©Carole Marsh/Gallopade International • www.gallopade.com • Willie gets wild about Weather!

Willie gets wild about Weather!

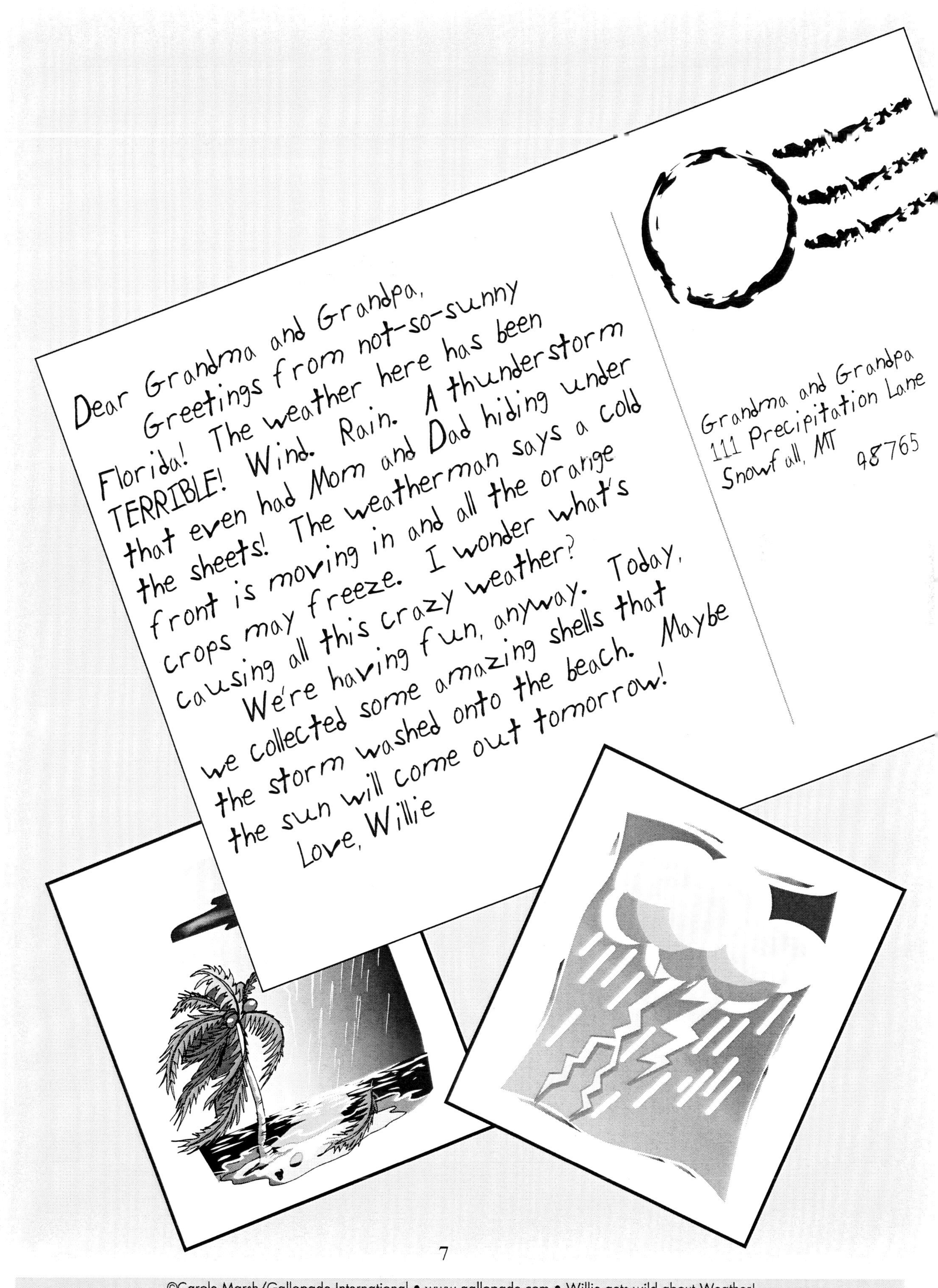

©Carole Marsh/Gallopade International • www.gallopade.com • Willie gets wild about Weather!

What is Weather?

***WIND!* Snow! RaiN!** Do any of those words come to mind when you think of weather? Actually, **weather** is a lot more complicated than just a raindrop falling to the ground. It's the state, or condition, of our atmosphere.

Think of the **atmosphere** as a protective cloak that surrounds Earth. What happens under that cloak is partly due to the sun, and the water cycle it creates. It's what we call weather.

Weather depends on many variables (changing conditions) such as temperature, moisture, wind velocity, and barometric pressure. The sun's energy in one part of the world might evaporate the water from nearby oceans and rivers, changing it into vapor. The atmosphere can transport that vapor to another location where, depending on the temperature, it might fall back to the ground as snow or rain.

The weather affects just about everything we do. Heavy rain might cancel your field trip. Hurricanes, tornadoes, and floods can cause massive damage. Droughts can kill crops we need for food!

Puzzle Time!

Find the following words in the word search below.

WORD BANK

water cycle
evaporate
liquid
drought
tornado
vapor
energy
atmosphere
oceans
hurricane

A T M O S P H E R E
D E E C H O Y C L H
I S V Q J G V C O U
U R H A R A Y D C R
Q H K E P C R O E R
I W N O R O Y M A I
L E R E U P R D N C
K O T G I J Q A S A
H A H B V S B W T N
W T O D A N R O T E

©Carole Marsh/Gallopade International • www.gallopade.com • Willie gets wild about Weather!

Climate Control!

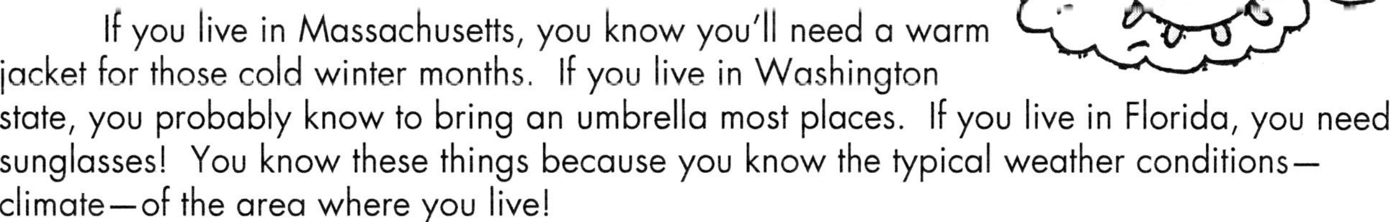

If you live in Massachusetts, you know you'll need a warm jacket for those cold winter months. If you live in Washington state, you probably know to bring an umbrella most places. If you live in Florida, you need sunglasses! You know these things because you know the typical weather conditions—climate—of the area where you live!

Climate is the average, or expected, weather conditions observed over a long period of time for a given area. Climates can change over time. Some of those changes are natural, and some are caused by man. Global warming is a climate change that affects the entire planet. The earth's temperature is gradually rising, and it has the potential to cause big problems: severe storms, drought, melting polar ice caps, and the extinction of some plants and animals.

Scientists aren't sure if global warming is a natural climate change, or if it is the result of people burning fossil fuels like oil and coal. The gases produced by burning fossil fuels escape into the air and heat the atmosphere.

Splish! Splash!

Don't you love to jump into puddles? **Perform the experiment below to see how weather affects puddles.**

Materials needed:

puddle   piece of chalk   sunny day

Instructions:

1. Pick a puddle on a driveway or sidewalk where you can draw with chalk.
2. Draw a circle around the puddle.
3. Two hours later, draw another circle around the edges of the puddle.
4. Continue drawing a new circle every couple of hours for the rest of the day.
5. What did the puddle do? Get larger? Get smaller? Stay the same? ________________

____

6. Do you think the weather affected your results? ________________

How? ____

____

©Carole Marsh/Gallopade International • www.gallopade.com • Willie gets wild about Weather!

Do you know how water gets into the atmosphere so it can fall as rain? It happens through a continuous process called the **water cycle**. The sun's heat causes water molecules from oceans, lakes, and rivers to change into air molecules, called **water vapor.** This vapor rises on winds into the atmosphere. When there is enough water vapor in the air, it falls back to the ground as rain.

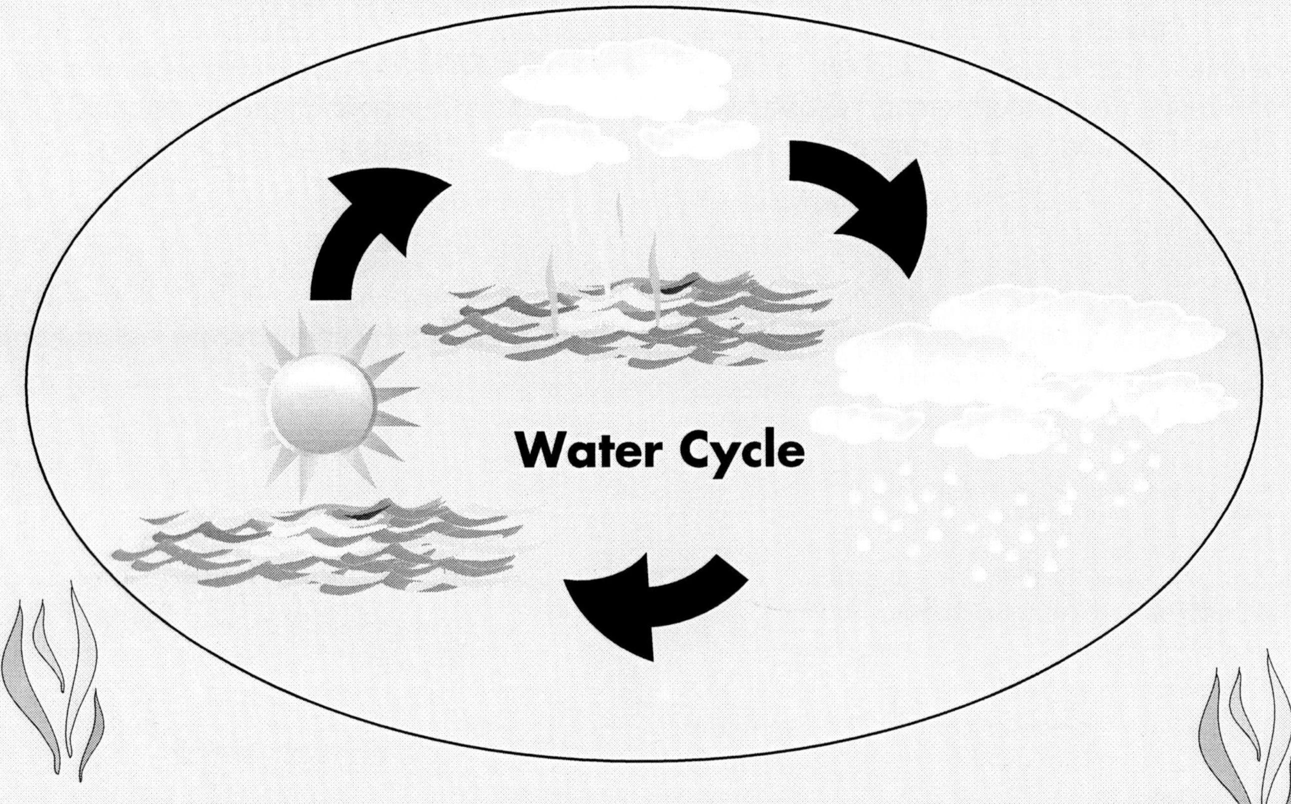

WORD DEFINITION
evaporate: to change from liquid to vapor

With so much of our planet's water in the oceans, it makes sense that most of the water that falls as rain comes from those oceans. As ocean water **evaporates**, it leaves the salt behind in the ocean and falls as fresh water.

Water evaporates all around the world. If it ends up high in the atmosphere where the temperature is colder, it condenses and turns from a gas to a liquid. The condensed water becomes water droplets clinging to dust particles in the air, and forms clouds or fog. If it's really cold, the water droplets freeze into water crystals.

When clouds are overloaded with water droplets or water crystals, the crystals or droplets fall to the ground in the form of rain or snow. When rain passes through air that is below freezing, it becomes sleet or hail.

©Carole Marsh/Gallopade International • www.gallopade.com • Willie gets wild about Weather!

All Steamed Up!

Water usually evaporates so slowly that it's impossible to see. You can speed up the process by heating up the water faster than the surrounding air heats, and watching water turn to vapor in the form of steam.

Be sure to have an adult help you with this experiment.

1. Add about 1/2-inch of water to a pot and put in on the stove.
2. Turn the stove on to medium heat, and watch as the water heats up.
3. When the water gets hot enough, you will see steam coming off the surface of the water. That's water vapor!

FAST FACT!

Raindrops fall between 7 and 18 miles per hour, depending on their size!

FAST FACT!

The wettest place in the United States is Mt. Wauakeake on the Hawaiian island of Kauai. It gets more than 37 feet of rainfall each year!

©Carole Marsh/Gallopade International • www.gallopade.com • Willie gets wild about Weather!

Currently, the Weather is Warm!

What keeps you warm in the winter and cool in the summer? The answer is **oceans**—even if you don't live near one! In the summer, oceans absorb a lot of the sun's heat, which cools the air. In the winter, oceans release heat into the atmosphere, warming the air.

The temperature of an ocean's water stays about the same most of the time. This helps prevent wild swings in the earth's temperature. All the oceans have hot spots created by the sun. These hot areas create currents—rivers of fast moving water—that spread heat throughout the ocean.

The most famous of all the currents is **El Niño** in the Pacific Ocean off South America. Normally, Pacific water currents change out warm surface water for cool, deep water. When wind doesn't blow the warm waters away from the land, cool water can't cycle in, and the waters stay warm. This causes El Niño.

El Niño changes weather patterns all around the Pacific, causing droughts in Australia, and excessive rain, and even hurricanes, on America's West Coast.

Time to Write!

Rappin' in the Ocean

Without the oceans, Earth's temperature would be wild.
Can you even imagine what that could do to you, child?
Without South Pacific currents, El Niño can appear,
Changing the weather for the worst, that's clear.

Create your own ocean rap below.

____

____

____

____

____

©Carole Marsh/Gallopade International • www.gallopade.com • Willie gets wild about Weather!

Getting To the Front

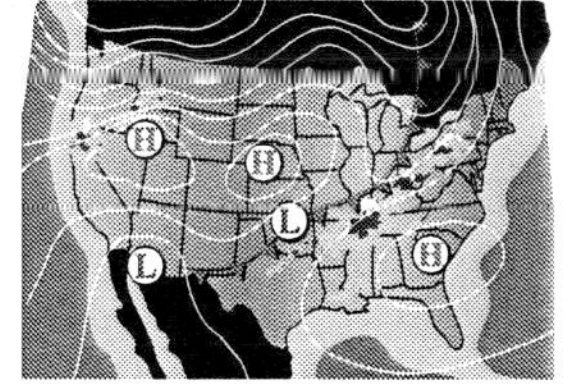

BAM! Imagine you're walking down the hall at school, not watching where you're going. **BAM!** You bump into someone else. Books go flying! That's what happens when two **air masses** try to occupy the same space at the same time. A collision of air masses can cause some pretty crazy weather.

An air mass is a huge pocket of air that has the same temperature and humidity. Depending on where it forms, an air mass can be cold and dry, or warm and humid.

A **cold front** occurs when a cold air mass collides with a warm air mass, causing the warm air to be pushed up. As the cold air mass moves, the water vapor condenses to form clouds. A cold front usually causes heavy rain, thunderstorms, or snow for a short time before it moves on. When a warm air mass moves over a cold air mass, it's called a **warm front**. A warm front can bring long-lasting rain or snow.

Scramble To the Front!

Unscramble the letters to figure out these weather words. Use the word bank below.

1. noisilcol ___ O ___ ___ ___ ___ ___ ___ ___ N
2. dmuitiyh ___ ___ M ___ ___ ___ T ___
3. ira sams ___ I ___ M ___ ___ ___
4. rmaw orntf ___ ___ ___ M ___ ___ ___ ___ ___
5. ruteearemept ___ ___ M ___ ___ ___ ___ ___ T ___ ___ ___
6. soedncnse ___ ___ ___ D ___ ___ ___ ___ ___

WORD BANK

humidity	air mass	condenses
warm front	collision	temperature

©Carole Marsh/Gallopade International • www.gallopade.com • Willie gets wild about Weather!

Creating Clouds!

If you live in the South, what's the first thing you notice when you step out of your air-conditioned house on a hot summer day? Sticky air! The name for that is **humidity**, and it's the amount of water vapor in the air. In the warm, wet South, you usually have high humidity. In the North, where it is cooler and dryer, you usually have low humidity.

Humidity can increase or decrease depending on the temperature. Humidity increases on a hot summer day in the North, because water in the area evaporates. More water vapor in the air means more humidity.

As humidity increases, **clouds** form. A cloud is nothing but condensed water on dust! Even though clouds look like soft cotton balls, they are very heavy. They stay up in the sky because their weight is spread out, and rising warm air currents keep them floating in the sky.

©Carole Marsh/Gallopade International • www.gallopade.com • Willie gets wild about Weather!

Have you ever noticed all the different kinds of clouds in the sky? **Cirrus** clouds float high in the atmosphere. They're thin, wispy, and long, and might mean the weather is changing. **Stratus** clouds cover the entire sky in a gray blanket. Prepare for a light drizzle when you see these!

The puffy cotton balls in the sky are **cumulus** clouds. As these clouds grow upward, they can turn into **cumulonimbus** clouds, which lead to thunderstorms! There are many other types of clouds. Some can be up to 50,000 feet tall. Fog is actually a cloud that forms on the ground!

It Sure is Cloudy in Here!

Create a cloud of your own with this experiment!
Be sure to have an adult help you.

Materials needed:
1 empty clear plastic 2-liter soda bottle (remove label)
1 sheet black construction paper
water
matches

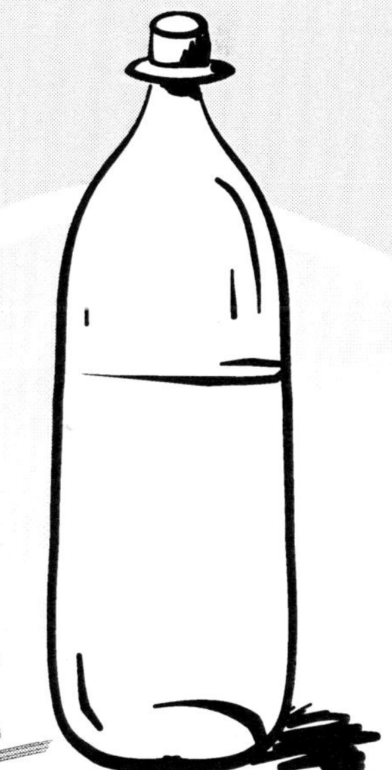

Instructions:

1. Pour 2 inches of very hot tap water into the 2-liter bottle.

2. Place your mouth over the opening and blow into it to ensure the bottle is fully expanded. Immediately seal the bottle tightly.

3. Shake the bottle vigorously for one minute. This will distribute water molecules in the air.

4. With adult supervision, light a match. Let it burn for two seconds, and then drop it into the bottle. Quickly recap the bottle.

5. Lay the bottle on its side with the black paper behind it. Press hard on the bottle for 10 seconds. The bottle is strong, so don't be afraid to push really hard. Release, observe, and repeat until a cloud forms.

6. When the cloud has formed, quickly unscrew the cap. You should see the cloud escape from the bottle. If not, give the bottle a light squeeze.

High humidity means a bad hair day for me!

©Carole Marsh/Gallopade International • www.gallopade.com • Willie gets wild about Weather!

Thunderstorms and Lightning! Frightening!

Thunderstorms are exciting and scary at the same time! Most thunderstorms occur during spring and summer, and they usually bring rain with them. And we're not talking about just a few drops! Some thunderclouds can dump several inches of rain an hour, and cause massive flooding. That's incredible, since it takes close to a million cloud droplets to make just one raindrop!

The friction created by air bouncing around in thunderclouds creates **lightning**. Did you know that lightning is a large surge of static electricity that goes from cloud to cloud, or from the cloud to the ground? The noise (thunder) you hear during a thunderstorm is caused by the intense heat created by the lightning. It makes the surrounding air expand, and then, **BOOM!**

Lightning is super-hot. In fact, just the air near a lightning bolt can be around 55,000°F. Lightning may be pretty, but it's also deadly. It often causes forest fires.

Think It Through

Answer the following questions from what you've learned so far. Circle the correct answer.

1. Most thunderstorms happen during the spring and fall.
   a. True b. False

2. During a thunderstorm, it can rain several _______ in a short time.
   a. feet
   b. inches
   c. drops

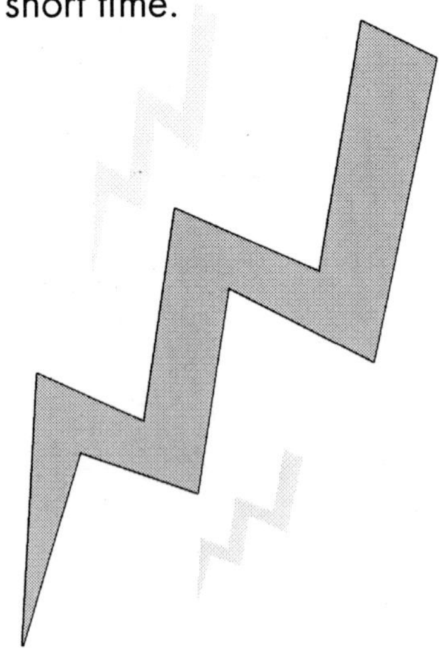

3. Thunder is caused by:
   a. clouds hitting each other
   b. lightning hitting the ground
   c. intense heat created by lightning

4. Lightning is:
   a. a large surge of static electricity
   b. a cold stream of light photons
   c. a word that means "to strike"

©Carole Marsh/Gallopade International • www.gallopade.com • Willie gets wild about Weather!

Cold as Ice!

Snowflakes come in some beautiful and amazing shapes! And did you know that no two are alike? Snowflakes form when the temperature nears freezing (32°F), and water droplets turn to ice crystals.

The more water that is added to the ice crystals, they larger they get. As the crystals start to fall, they hit other crystals and, soon, snowflakes form. If it is warmer by the ground, the snowflakes melt a little as they fall and turn into sleet and freezing rain, which can then lead to dangerous ice storms.

Snow is fun, but it can also be hazardous. Blizzards damage electrical power lines, and bury cars and even trains! Heavy snow and strong winds can create a whiteout. In a whiteout, you lose all sense of where things are. You can't tell the ground from the sky, or how far or near something is to you. When you hear that a blizzard is coming, you should stay inside where it's warm and safe!

Snow Art!

Create snowflakes of your own in the spaces below. Remember that no two are alike!

©Carole Marsh/Gallopade International • www.gallopade.com • Willie gets wild about Weather!

Hurricanes and Tornadoes

If you've ever tried to throw a ball or a Frisbee on a windy day, you know that a little wind can cause big problems. Really strong winds, like the ones that accompany hurricanes and tornadoes, can be deadly!

Hurricanes are powerful storms that form over water. The center of a hurricane is called the "eye." It carries winds up to 200 miles an hour, along with heavy rain. Once the eye reaches land, a hurricane can cause extreme flooding and wind damage.

Tornadoes are dangerous, too. Their spinning, funnel-shaped clouds are not as wide as a hurricane, but they can drop out of the sky at wind speeds up to 300 miles an hour. You can't predict exactly where a tornado will touch down, but wherever that is, you'll find a path of destruction. ***YIKES!***

Bubble Time!

Fill in the bubblegram using the words below.

hurricane   destruction   rain   thunderstorms   powerful

1. O __ __ E __ __ __ __ __
2. T __ O __ __ __ __ __ S __ __ __ __ __ __
3. __ A __ O
4. __ E __ __ __ __ __ O __ __ __ __ __
5. O __ __ R __ __ __ __ __ __ __

Use the bubble letters to fill in the missing word below.

Tornadoes pack a powerful ____________________.

©Carole Marsh/Gallopade International • www.gallopade.com • Willie gets wild about Weather!

Wet or Dry?

Have you ever been really thirsty and then drank too much? It makes your stomach hurt! That's a lot like what happens when an area gets a lot more or a lot less water than normal. It can make things very uncomfortable!

When an area that normally gets a sufficient amount of rain each year suddenly gets very little rain, it's called a **drought**. Without enough rain, crops don't grow well, and water sources dry up. Droughts create dry, brittle vegetation, which can be fuel for forest fires. In some areas of the world, a drought can also cause famine—an extreme lack of food—because of ruined crops.

Too much rain can be just as harmful as too little rain. **Flooding** occurs when streams, rivers, lakes, and the ground can no longer hold all the rainwater. Floods can rip out crops and lift houses off their foundations!

Really heavy rain that falls very quickly can create a flash flood. Flash floods happen so fast that most people aren't ready for them. They can also cause mudslides, which destroy houses in a matter of minutes.

Secret Message!

Use the code below to figure out the secret message!

©Carole Marsh/Gallopade International • www.gallopade.com • Willie gets wild about Weather!

It's All in How You Measure

Have you ever wondered how people predict the weather? **Meteorology** is the study of weather, and the scientists who study meteorology are called **meteorologists**. It's a fancy name for "weatherman!"

Meteorologists predict the weather by measuring it! An important tool in measuring the weather is a **barometer**, which reads air pressure. An increase in a barometer's air pressure reading occurs before cold air moves in, and we know that cold air has low humidity. So, what does that tell us? It tells us there is likely to be low humidity and no chance for rain. It's a perfect day for a field trip!

A decrease in a barometer's air pressure reading tells us that warm, humid air is arriving and there's a chance for rain. Bring your umbrella!

Picture This!

Draw and color a picture showing what the weather might look like on a day when the barometer shows a decrease in air pressure. Be sure to draw yourself in the picture, dressed for the day!

Tools and Equipment

Performing experiments requires the use of some special tools and equipment. Some of the tools and equipment used to study weather are:

Anemometers measure wind speed. 

Barometers measure air pressure, which is referred to as barometric pressure. 

Wind socks and vanes measure wind direction.

Thermometers measure air temperature.

Hygrometers measure humidity. 

Tool Time!

Use the weather tools in the word bank to solve this crossword puzzle!

Across

3. You'll always know which way the wind is blowing!

4. Pressure's low!

5. It's getting hot and sticky in here!

Down

1. What's the temperature?

2. Is it kite-flying weather?

Word Bank

anemometer
hygrometer
thermometer
barometer
wind sock

©Carole Marsh/Gallopade International • www.gallopade.com • Willie gets wild about Weather!

Someday, I'll Have a Cool Job!

World's Smartest Boss

Meteorologists specialize in studying weather and weather patterns.

Radar technicians repair weather radar systems.

Satellite technicians build and repair weather satellites.

Weather observers collect information about weather and sea conditions for use by meteorologists.

Fire weather forecasters predict wind and rain conditions to help firefighters battle wildfires.

What do you like?

Which career appeals to you? ______________________________

Why? ____

____

____

©Carole Marsh/Gallopade International • www.gallopade.com • Willie gets wild about Weather!

Have you ever thought about being an inventor? Have you watched a show on TV where someone showed his invention to the world? How can you become an inventor?

All of us create or invent something at some time in our lives. Usually, it's something we use to fix a problem. However, for you to achieve the status of a "true inventor," you must be able to go beyond the ordinary!

Did you know that not all scientists graduated from college? Some, like Thomas Edison, didn't even go to school. They taught themselves by reading everything they could on subjects they liked. There are certain attributes that make a person successful. Do you know what those attributes are?

The Right Stuff!

Circle the following words that play an important role in achieving success.

PATIENCE WISDOM

MISTAKES FAILURE LAZINESS

ENCOURAGEMENT

PERSEVERANCE GIVING UP

TIME EXCUSES WHINING

OPTIMISM BRAINSTORMING

©Carole Marsh/Gallopade International • www.gallopade.com • Willie gets wild about Weather!

Aristotle was a Greek philosopher who lived more than 2,000 years ago! He tried to prove that air has no weight.

Gabriel Fahrenheit was a German scientist who lived from 1686 to 1736. He developed many meteorological instruments, including thermometers. Our system of measuring temperature is named for him.

Evangelista Torricelli was an Italian physicist and mathematician who lived from 1608 to 1647. He invented the barometer, an instrument still used today to measure air pressure.

William Ferrel was an American meteorologist who lived from 1817 to 1891. He studied the effects of weather on the tides for the U.S. Coast Guard.

John Coleman is an American news weathercaster who was born in 1934. He founded The Weather Channel.

Who Did What?

Draw a line to match the scientists below with their discoveries.

1. Aristotle — a. 

2. Gabriel Fahrenheit — b.

3. Evangelista Torricelli — c. 

4. William Ferrel — d.

5. John Coleman — e.

©Carole Marsh/Gallopade International • www.gallopade.com • Willie gets wild about Weather!

The Scientific Method

Scientists use the scientific method to explore observations and answer questions about why something happens the way it does. They make a prediction about something and then design experiments to prove or disprove their idea, or **hypothesis**.

To make the scientific method work for you, follow the steps below to construct a hypothesis, design an experiment, and to perform and evaluate your experiment. Just like for a scientist, the scientific method helps you focus your questions about your idea. When you consistently get the same results from your experiments, your hypothesis becomes a **theory**. A theory is an idea or belief about something you've arrived at through experimentation.

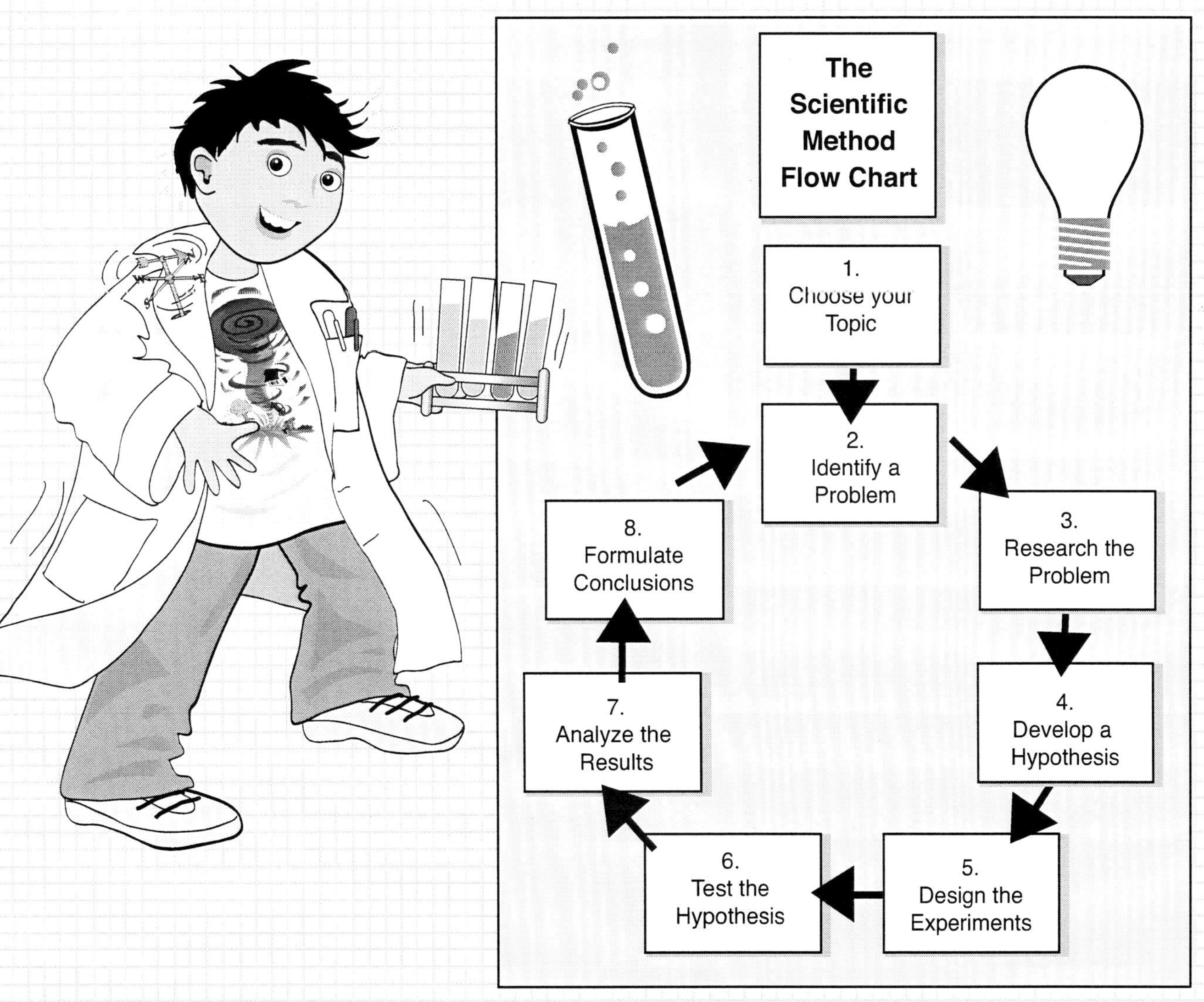

©Carole Marsh/Gallopade International • www.gallopade.com • Willie gets wild about Weather!

Blowing in the Wind

Hypothesis:

To find out if objects interrupt the wind's direction.

Objective:

To observe and record the wind's direction at various points around a building.

Materials:

small container of bubbles
a drawing of the outside of your house and the area surrounding it
notepad with two columns, titled "Area" and "Direction," and lines marked 1 through 10
compass

Method:

1. On a windy day, take your materials outside of your house to an open space with nothing nearby.
2. Use the notepad to describe your location compared to your house, and to note the wind's compass reading. Use terms like, "in the open back yard," or "at the south corner of the house" to describe your location.
3. Find and mark your location on your drawing as #1.
4. Record your location in your notepad on line 1 to match your drawing's location number.
5. Position your house drawing on the ground so that it matches the direction your house is facing.
6. Using the compass, find north, then mark north, south, east, and west on your house drawing.
7. Hold the compass in one hand and blow a long stream of bubbles.

©Carole Marsh/Gallopade International • www.gallopade.com • Willie gets wild about Weather!

8. Using the compass, take a wind direction reading of the bubbles' path and mark the compass direction on your notepad under the Direction column.
9. Repeat steps 3-8 nine more times at different locations and distances around the house. Try standing close to the house, at the corners of the house, and near a tree. Don't forget to match the location you put on your drawing to the line you enter on the notepad.

Results:

1. What patterns did you notice in the bubbles as the wind blew them?

____

____

____

2. Did the wind blow in the same direction all around your house?

____

3. Did where you stood make a difference in the direction the bubbles blew? ________________

4. What direction did the bubbles go when you blew them toward the house? ________________

5. What do you think might happen if you tried this experiment on another day? ______________

6. Was your hypothesis correct? ________________

7. Turn to page 28 and answer the questions.

©Carole Marsh/Gallopade International • www.gallopade.com • Willie gets wild about Weather!

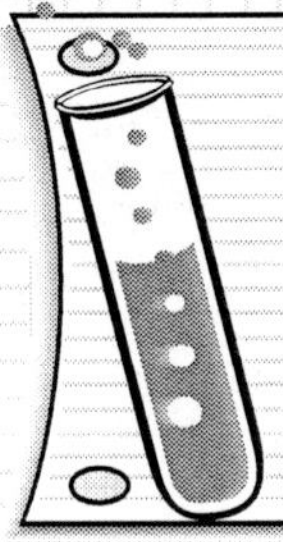

What Did I Learn?

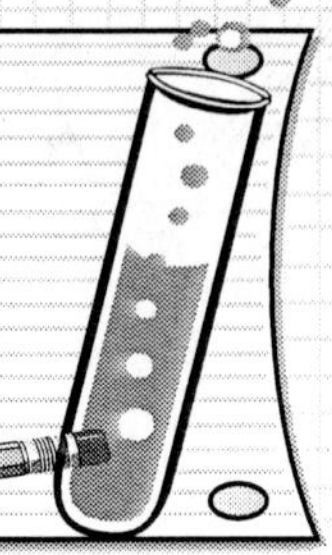

Here's your chance to describe what you learned in your science fair experiment!

1. When I started my project, what was I trying to find out?

____

____

____

2. What were my actual results?

____

____

____

3. Did my research method give me quality results? Why or why not?

____

____

____

4. What would I do differently if I did this project again?

____

____

____

©Carole Marsh/Gallopade International • www.gallopade.com • Willie gets wild about Weather!

Join the Science Alliance

Join the Science Alliance by raising your right hand and saying the pledge below.

Science Alliance Pledge:

I, ____________________________, agree to pay attention to... learn about... learn to love... learn to use... learn to share... good science in school and my daily life so that others and I may benefit from more knowledge and skill in this important subject. I also agree to accept the idea that it is better to have knowledge and never need to use it, than to not have knowledge and need to use it.

____

Sign your name here.

©Carole Marsh/Gallopade International • www.gallopade.com • Willie gets wild about Weather!

Metric Conversions

Conversions To Metric Measures

Symbol	When You Know	Multiply By	To Find	Symbol
		LENGTH		
in	inches	25.4	millimeters	mm
ft	feet	0.305	meters	m
yd	yards	0.914	meters	m
mi	miles	1.61	kilometers	km
		AREA		
in^2	square inches	645.2	square millimeters	mm^2
ft^2	square feet	0.093	square meters	m^2
yd^2	square yard	0.836	square meters	m^2
ac	acres	0.405	hectares	ha
mi^2	square miles	2.59	square kilometers	km^2
		VOLUME		
fl oz	fluid ounces	29.57	milliliters	mL
gal	gallons	3.785	liters	L
ft^3	cubic feet	0.028	cubic meters	m^3
yd^3	cubic yards	0.765	cubic meters	m^3
		MASS		
oz	ounces	28.35	grams	g
lb	pounds	0.454	kilograms	kg
T	short tons (2000 lb)	0.907	megagrams (or "metric ton")	Mg (or "t")
		TEMPERATURE		
°F	Fahrenheit	1. Subtract 32 from Fahrenheit number 2. Multiply answer by 5 3. Divide answer by 9	Celsius	°C

©Carole Marsh/Gallopade International • www.gallopade.com • Willie gets wild about Weather!

Glossary

air mass: a large body of air that has similar temperature and humidity throughout

climate: the pattern of weather an area experiences over a long period of time

condensation: the process by which a gas changes into a liquid

current: a stream of water that flows like a river through the ocean

front: a place where two air masses meet

humidity: a measurement of the amount of water vapor in the air

meteorology: the study of weather

precipitation: water that falls from clouds to the earth

water cycle: the constant movement of water from Earth's surface to the atmosphere and back to the Earth's surface

water vapor: the gas form of water

weather: the condition of the atmosphere at a certain place and time

©Carole Marsh/Gallopade International • www.gallopade.com • Willie gets wild about Weather!

Answer Key

Page 13
1. collision; 2. humidity; 3. air mass 4. warm front; 5. temperature; 6. condenses

Page 16
1. b; 2. b; 3. c; 4. a

Page 18
1. powerful; 2. thunderstorms; 3. rain; 4. destruction; 5. hurricane
Bubble word: punch

Page 19
Never cross moving water!

Page 21

Across	Down
3. wind sock	1. thermometer
4. barometer	2. anemometer
5. hygrometer	

Page 23
patience, wisdom, mistakes, failure, encouragement, perseverance, time, optimism, brainstorming

Page 24
1. d; 2. b; 3. e; 4. a; 5. c

©Carole Marsh/Gallopade International • www.gallopade.com • Willie gets wild about Weather!